Never Too Early to Dream
Big

Never Too Early to Dream
Big

Hope and Dreams of
Young Philadelphia Authors

Brought to you by:

Authentic Publishing LLC

www.AuthenticPublishingLLC.com

Authentic Publishing LLC books may be purchased for business or educational use. For information, please write to Authentic Publishing LLC at the above address, or contact Authentic Publishing LLC through the above website.

ISBN 978-0-9843577-1-0

FIRST EDITION

Introduction

Children should have no ceilings or parameters when it comes to what they aspire to be. Each child has a God given gift to see the world as it is through their eyes while focusing on becoming positive influences on the future.

Authentic Publishing LLC gave several Philadelphia public school children the opportunity to write a short story, essay, or poem about what they aspire to be. In return, we got much more. We received a plethora of works ranging from children's insight on world issues to premature struggles with life.

We are honored to publish these K-8 works and amazed at these youths' creativity. Authentic Publishing LLC hopes that by publishing these works, we help keep the youth, in Philadelphia and around the world, inspired to dream big.

Authentic Publishing LLC

A DIFFERENT ME

OLD ME, NEW ME
HAPPY ME, SAD ME
ALL ABOUT ME
NEVER ABOUT YOU
ALL WHAT I WANT
NOT WHAT I NEED
BUT NOW I ASPIRE TO BE
A DIFFERENT ME

TO CARE AND TO HELP
TO BE THERE
WHEN YOU NEED A FRIEND
TO LEND A HAND
WHEN YOU ONLY GOT TWO
BE HAPPY FOR ME
AND I'LL BE HAPPY FOR YOU

OLD ME, NEW ME
I ASPIRE TO BE
A DIFFERENT ME

FELICIA G.

Goals

When I grow up, I have many goals in life. I want to live to succeed all my goals and also invest in life.

My first goal is to go to college because my life would be so much better if I go to college. I want to go to Louisville. I want to go to Louisville because it has a nice campus, basketball team and it is real far away from my family, but I don't want to be far away from my family.

My second goal after going to college is to go to the NBA, because I have the height, the Athletic Skills and the potential to go to the NBA. I also want to live my dreams being in the Hall-of Fame and win a couple of Championships with the Philadelphia Sixers.

My goal is to retire from the NBA after playing for twelve years, because I do not want to spend my whole life in the NBA. I want to get married someday.

These are my goals for a positive future and for real life. Never give up on your dreams is what I have always heard.

Tyquaan B.

Earth

People wonder,

People ponder,

About the future of our earth

Violence, pollution, war & peace,

Swine flu, checks fly through

Economy crashing, bills flashing

Hunger slashing, lives at stake

Animals dying, souls flying,

Darkness is rising........

Huh it was just a dream......

Matthew B. and Randi C.

When I Grow Up

I have many goals in life but my main goals are to go to law school, have kids and be happily married.

When I grow up, I want to live in New York City. The reason why I want to live there is because they have good law schools. New York City has a lot more things and career places up there that people can choose from.

Then when I move up to New York City, I want to go to law school. I always dreamed of being a lawyer. I want to be a lawyer because I want to get all the bad people off the streets. I want to help people get their justice if they were a victim to crime.

My last goal is to have kids and be happily married. I want to have twins and be married to a hard working man. I want to have a boy and girl as twins.

These are my lifelong goals for when I grow up. Being in Law School, living in New York City and being happily married with twins a boy and a girl.

Mykia G.

College

I have many goals. One goal includes going to college. I want to have kids and a husband. Also I want to be a pediatrician, have a big house for my family to live in, a nice car.

The reason I want to go to college is because I want to be successful. I want to work in the medical field. You have to do at least seven years of college. I think that college would be fun. You can meet new people and you don't have to go home afterwards. But it might be hard because you are going to have to keep up with everything. You are also going to have keep focused because of all the parties and everything.

Then after I finish school, I want to become a pediatrician. The main reason I want to become a pediatrician is that I like to help people, especially kids. They are just so cute. But it takes such a long time to be what you want. I think I would get out of school when I am about twenty eight. Wow!! But I also like working with babies and finding out new things.

Now after I get out of school, I want to get married to a successful man. I would like for him to be a doctor or a lawyer. Then after a year or so, I want to have kids. First, I want a boy because I think he might be easier to take care of. Next, I want a girl because I want to spoil her and get her everything she wants. A while after that, I want to have three more children.

Last but not least, I need a home for my family to live in. I am not sure where I want to live yet. But I think I want to live in the suburbs. I want to have three nice cars, and I want my husband to have three nice cars also.

These are the goals that I have when I grow up. First go to college, then be a pediatrician, have a family with nice cars and a house.

Salimatou

A Couple Ideas

I have a couple goals for my life at this moment, a couple ideas. When I grow up, I want to be a writer. The reason why I want to be a writer is because I love to write, and I love reading interesting books. I also know there are some kids out there interested in the same stuff, so, I want to write a book that people my age will like.

If I don't become a writer, I want to own a daycare. The reason is because I know there are thousands of adults that want to go out and have fun. They want to just get away and leave their kids behind. So, I will get paid good money for taking care of them.

If I don't own a daycare, I want to become a private investigator. The reason why is because I like figuring out crimes, along with going to college this will help me get everything that I want to get out of life.

Last but not least, I want to be a veterinarian and help animals. The reason why is because I love animals, and don't like seeing them hurt.

When I grow up, I want a faithful marriage, two kids and a big house with lots of money, and, in order to have all these, I have to work two jobs which are two of my goals.

These are some of my goals and what I want to do, so I hope you enjoyed reading.

Darian A.

Dream Rap

I want to be a pilot and fly overseas.

I want to help you achieve your dreams.

I wish to be a rescue pilot saving some lives.

I wish to help injured troops flying through the skies.

I will go to college and probably the army.

I'll avoid those drugs and won't mess up my life.

How about you, will you be all right?

Emil G.

WHEN I GROW UP

When I grow up I have many goals. These goals include being a nurse, having three children and moving to New Jersey. These are my three top goals because I think I can make them come true. I have always wanted to be a nurse, move to New Jersey and have three children.

I want to be a nurse when I grow up because I want to help people, I am a good listener and I can catch on fast. I was also thinking of being a Pediatrician because I love working with children, but I really want to be a nurse.

When I grow up, I want to have three children. I want to have two girls and a boy. I want to have three children because I think that is a good amount of children to have. I love children very much, that is why I want to have three.

I want to live in New Jersey when I grow up. I want to live in New Jersey because I think it is a good place to live. I also want to move to New Jersey because I don't want to move to far away from my family. If I live in New Jersey, I don't think that I would have a lot of problems. I can't wait to move to New Jersey.

These are my three top goals that I want to make in life. If I do make my goals come true, I'm going to be the luckiest person in the world. Also, if I do make my goals come true, I am going to be so happy. But I really hope I become a nurse the most. I really want to be a nurse because I really like helping people.

Tierra N.

My Essay

When I grow up, I want to start my life with these goals. I want to finish school and college. By the time I make it out of college, I want a successful career to keep me on my feet. Then, when I am paid, I want to move to Florida and I want a family.

Before I become an adult, I want to finish school and college so I can get whatever job I want. I want to go to college down south because it seems to be a lot calmer down there.

Then, I want a husband. I just might have kids even though that's my fear, but I don't know what the future holds. By the way, I want a tough fine smart man. I want to live in a big house with a happy life, and I want my family to be happy too. I hope I never lose them.

Maigan S.

How I Became a Better Aunt

A few months earlier, I wasn't such a good role model for my three-year-old niece. What I mean by this is that I used to argue and get jealous of her. Yeah, you are probably saying, "With a three year old?" Well, yes. This is how it all started. As soon as Imani moved in with us, she thought she was the boss and she was really disrespecting me.

I was jealous and mad, and every time I would yell at her for being bad, my mom and dad would think that she was innocent and didn't do anything. Can you believe that?

Then I began to realize that I was not the baby of the family anymore, Imani was. That upset me. Right away, I knew that we were going to have problems -- we fought all the time.

Then one day, I said enough is enough! I am the aunt and Imani is going to learn to respect me. Knowing Imani, I knew it was going to be tricky. I had to learn to have patience with her. She is very stubborn. It took a long time to get her to listen and learn manners. It also took a long time to set a good example.

I am still trying very hard to stay positive and have patience with Imani.

Since she has been with us, I have learned to get to know her more and now we respect one another. I don't have any problems with her now. I take her everywhere. I love to baby sit Imani because she listens, has manners and is well behaved.

Now, I can say that she is my favorite niece and I am her favorite auntie. Imani deserves the best and she has it and I am going to keep it that way.

Margaret J.

My Aspiration

I aspire to help people with the children that they can't take care of. I aspire to help the people that feel as though they have no other place to turn after they had a baby. Babies' lives are precious, and they deserve to live.

I want to help anyone who wants to abort their kids just because they don't have any money, a house or food. I have no problem or grudges with people who abort their children but I have a special wish in my heart that they will stop.

I love all children whether they're my little brother or somebody else's child. I aspire to grow up and be successful and help all pregnant people who are in trouble, with no money or support. By doing this I could be saving the next doctor, lawyer, or the next person to find the cure for HIV/AIDS or Cancer.

That is my aspiration in life.

Whitney D.

People Will Call Me Doctor

My name is Quaniece. I want to be a pediatrician and help kids. I want to have two kids, a boy and a girl. I want to move to Miami where it is sunny and hot.

I want to be a pediatrician because I love kids. I want to help kids and save their lives. I want to go to Spellman college. When I graduate, I want to have my own office, and by that time people will call me Doctor.

Then, I will move to Miami, because it is hot and you get to be in the sun, no coldness in the air. I would love that for me and my kids.

Quaniece

Three Goals

My three goals I want to accomplish is going to a great college, living in California, and working for the military in the medical field. I really hope to accomplish them.

Before I get a job, I want to go to college, a great college. I want to study about the medical field and art for fun. Going to college would make my family proud because I have reached one out of two goals so far. It would make me proud of myself also because I finished something I thought I never would accomplish.

Hopefully when I finish college, I can move to California and get a nice house in a nice neighborhood. Then, I would start making plans for working for the military in the medical field, because that is what I hope to do for a job. This would also mean I finished two out of the three goals in my life.

Working for the military in the medical area would mean a lot to me. I made up this goal when I was watching the show "House," but the military part I got from my dad because he always talked about how wild and dangerous I am. I want to work there for thirty years and then retire. After I retire, this means that I have finished all three of my goals.

When I finish all three of these goals, my life will be perfect.

Krystal C.

Why you ask?

When I grow up, my goal is to play for the Los Angeles Lakers, in the NBA, live in LA on top of a hill, have two kids and a wife and make enough money to support my family.

The first goal that I want to accomplish is to go to the NBA and play for the Los Angeles Lakers and wear the number one. Why? My favorite number is number one and my third favorite player is on that team, Kobe Bryant. The positions that I want to play are point guard and shooting guard.

My second goal is to be a billion air with lots of cars, courts, pools and theaters inside. The house will have five bedrooms and two dirt bikes.

Why you ask again? I like cool cars, playing ball, swimming, and watching movies.

One of my other goals is to have a boy, a girl and a wife. I want my first child to be a boy and my second one to be a girl because she will have an older brother who will be able to protect her. The reason I want a wife is because she will be able help me relax, love me, and rub my muscles when I come home from road games and practice.

My Dream

My dream is to become a teacher when I grow up. I want to help kids get a very good education. I also want to help kids make good decisions because I usually see or hear kids making bad choices. For example, I heard about kids taking a gun to school. I want to convince kids that is not a good idea.

I have to go to college first though, and I am only in the fourth grade. So that means I still have a long way to go until I become a teacher. Even though I have a long way to go, I know I can make it, and I have supportive role models to help me along the way.

Taylor S.

My Future

When I grow up, I want to be an FBI agent. I want to be an FBI agent because I get to make this dangerous world safer, although I might have to use weapons, like pistols, shotguns, machine guns and gas grenades to do it. The cool part is that I will get to use cool gadgets like a key that opens all doors and C4 charges.

Some information might be so top secret that I will not be able to tell the public. I will be solving and investigating crimes and mysteries most of the time. I will also make a high salary.

I have to go to college for four years so I can do all of this. I also have to train and exercise every day. That is why I want to be a FBI agent.

Adam Z.

Why won't it stop?

Terrorism, terrorism

That's all you think about

It makes you wonder what life

Would be like

Without.

This need's to stop

Before it spreads

Because of this many are

Dead.

Every day and night

This happens

And it's just a fright.

Presidents do the best they can

To try to help

With this situations' plans.

Hope, hope

When will it come?

All these people are sitting so

Glum!

Hopefully

Terrorism will leave and we can finally follow our

Dream.

Even though terrorism is still here I have a dream it will disappear!

Abigail B.

What Would I Be When I Grow Up?

I think I know what I would want to be when I grow up. I am planning to be a soccer player because my favorite thing to do is sports and my favorite sport is soccer. I will try to be the best soccer player ever. Then I will try to win!

When the people watch the game, they won't fight, and when I get paid, I am going to give my money to the poor people.

Or K.

Never Too Early To Dream Big

The plan for my life is to be a chef and feed homeless children and adults all over the world. I will also feed homeless animals that live on the streets. This will help them so they don't die from hunger.

I like this because I think it is important for animals and humans to live as long as they can. I have had this dream since I was four, and I will have it in the future!

I have had difficulties in my life, like not being able to see my biological parents. I think animals and humans need love and care. That's where I am willing to help.

Sarah C.

My Future

In the future, my dream is to become a professional skateboarder. I will be in the videos and competitions. I know that I am off to a good start at this career because on April 18th, I entered a competition with 150 kids and got third place. Not only did I win a lot of stuff, but I got sponsored by a company. I want this career because it's a lot of fun and I could get a good paycheck.

It is also fun to speed down a hill feeling the wind blown in your face and not think about all the troubles in life. I ignore the economy, wars and child abductions. Skateboarding helps me to keep my mind off that. That is why I want to be a pro skateboarder!!!

David S.

My Dream

I have a dream to be a teacher. I want to be a teacher because I want the children to be great citizens and make good choices. I know what it's like to teach because I like to teach my brother and sister multiplication.

Even though I am only in fourth grade, I have eight more years of school and then college, so I have a long time until it happens. I will be very happy if I get that job because it sounds exciting! Another reason I want to be a teacher is so that I can learn more about my students.

It would be so much fun to be a teacher.

Brianna A.

World

Fear is near, fear is here,

People bleed, people tear,

War is poor, for some it's more,

Why the bother,

When you hurt my father,

I hope it ends,

So my friends,

Can see them once again

By Khaled Z. and Damon P.

Cancer Poem

Even though there is no cure for cancer in this world, I have a dream that someday there will be a cure found for all types!

So many types of cancer

And still no cure

So many people have it

I am not sure

What to do or what to say

How to have fun or play

When I know people are dying

And there is not much for me to do

I can donate money

But that's about all I can do.

Now there is bladder and breast

Colon and rectal

Endometrial and kidney

Leukemia and lung

Melanoma and lymphoma

Pancreatic and prostate

Skin and thyroid

That is all I can name

But I am sure there is more

What a terrible thing this cancer is

And still no cure.

Megan M.

We Need A Cure

The world is not at its best right now. For example, economics, poverty, and war are on everyone's mind. Another thing that makes the world a terrible place to live is people dying from cancer. Even though there are many deaths from this disease, there is still no cure, I have a dream that one day there will be one.

Over the years there have been many conflicts about whether or not there will ever be a cure for the many types of cancer. Some of these are lung and skin cancer. Some people think it is unrealistic that there will ever be a cure. However others have struggled their whole life hoping and believing that one day a cure will be reality. There is research going on all the time to help the dream come true. Even President Obama has pledged to conquer cancer in our time. He has promised six billion dollars for cancer research. However, most cancer researchers do not believe that all cancers will have a cure, but they hope that all will become treatable.

One really bad type of cancer that has no cure is skin cancer or melanoma. Many people get this by being in the sun often. It can spread throughout the body extremely quickly and is very deadly. If someone gets a new mole that appears irregularly, it can turn out to be melanoma.

Another type of cancer is lung cancer. One of the most common causes of this is smoking. This cancer starts in the tissues of the lungs and then slowly spreads in the body. This spreads slower than other cancers. Lung cancer causes breathing problems. I would never want to have lung cancer or any other type of cancer. I especially know what cancer can do because my dad recently died from melanoma and my grandmother died from lung cancer. It would mean so much to me, as well as the rest of the world if doctors and scientist could find a cure.

We can help by donating money to research and praying for a cure.

I still have a dream that one day there will be a cure for cancer. I don't know how long it will take, but I will never lose hope. I know that eventually there will be one, so there can be less sadness in the world. Hopefully during my life time, they will finally find a cure for cancer!

Chelsea T.

Singer

I would like to be a singer to help give money to sick children with cancer and other sicknesses. Also I would give them back stage passes, tickets to concerts, and a chance to hang out with me. And I would never stop giving them these gifts.

Erin G.

Regret

Why did I ever go to sleep so late?

Last night I thought to myself the driver will wait.

But I had to walk all the way to school.

I could have been on the bus, instead of looking like a
fool.

Why did I ever stop studying for my test?

I tried pretty hard, but I did not do my best.

All I got was a C, my worst grade yet.

Not studying for my test, that's what I regret.

Why did I eat that Christmas Cane?

Now my tooth hurts, and I'm in so much pain.

I wish I didn't have that sugary sweet.

But what can I say now; I'm in the dentist's seat.

Why did I forget to clean my room?

Now I'm left by myself, with a sponge and a broom.

And my mother spent an hour yelling at me.

I regret so many things as you can see.

Olga S.

Anne Frank

June 12 Birthday

Knowing that tomorrow, she may not see the day,

Asking if she'll ever stop being treated this way.

Hardship after hardship, she ran through them all,

But this girl got up, and she stood strong and tall.

Yet this child suffered for so many years,

Inside her soul, there were mostly fears.

Waiting for the wars to cease,

Wishing for some worldwide peace.

All she had with her was her diary and hope,

Watching as relatives were killed, tied to a rope.

And to think she could have been here today,

If only the Nazis didn't treat her this way.

Lets all remember the spirit she had,

She died so suddenly, oh how so sad.

Olga S

America the Brave

Through World War I, and World War II

They fought for me and fought for you.

And even way back to the Revolutionary war

They pointed their guns, until their fingers were sore.

They fought for our justice and our rights

Victory comes through battles and fights.

And to this day we raise our flags high

We remember those brave men, and try not to cry.

Olga S.

Christmas Time

Christmas is a time of joy and gladness.

Family and friends gather together.

In this time of cold weather,

A sound of joy and laughter

A sound of peace

A few songs and presents

That's a thing of peace.

Kathlynne F.

I Love You Mom

I love you mom when I'm asleep,

And when I'm awake,

And when the sun rises in the morning,

And I will end the day as a hug and a kiss,

Till tomorrow, I love you mom.

Katlynne F.

A special first grader from the Philadelphia area,
has contributed a short tale about a turkey in Hawaii.

The turkey went to (Hawaii) His name was Mote. The volcano exploded. Then the ground shook. Then a earthquake appeared. Mote was scared. He ran as fast as his little legs could

carry him. The sand
crunched when the
people ran. But
everybody was ok
until it exploded
again.

The End

www.ingramcontent.com/pod-product-compliance
Lightning Source LLC
LaVergne TN
LVHW011412080426
835511LV00005B/504